I0483035

raspberry colored scars

raspberry colored scars

elisabeth foster

NEW DEGREE PRESS

COPYRIGHT © 2019 ELISABETH FOSTER

All rights reserved.

RASPBERRY COLORED SCARS

ISBN   978-1-64137-321-0 *Paperback*

         978-1-64137-622-8 *Ebook*

to the friend who told me
erase it from your mind
make it go away
that is all you can do
it didn't go away

this is for you
and anyone who tried to erase
what is forever engrained in them

this is for us

contents

acknowledgements

my first love
is mine
he is my father
who taught me
compassion lies within the heart

always within
yourself

my mother is
the toughest I have ever known
she gives strength
and power to me
shows me beauty
is different to all

but love is the same

my grandmother
taught me to write
she looks down on me
smiling
knowing we are together
in these pages

I feel you with me

in this journey
I am not alone
my family and friends
stand by me

I am grateful
for the strength you've given
and the support you've provided

you know who you are

from the author

I see my life in flashes of color
this part of my life,
that I am choosing to share with you,
is red

red is the color of love, passion, deep emotion;
it is also the color of blood, scars, and pain

I hope that you feel with me
in a way that is suited to your needs and experiences
and I hope that you can heal
in the way that I still am

you may read things you don't want to read, and feel things you
don't want to feel
but this needs to be read, and it needs to be felt

I hope that you can understand what I have been through is not unique
but it is important and real

know that in reading this
you are connecting with those around you, with me and with yourself

know that in feeling this
you are not alone

"And the air was full of Thoughts and Things to Say. But at times like these, only the Small Things are ever said. Big Things lurk unsaid inside."

–ARUNDHATI ROY, *THE GOD OF SMALL THINGS*

"The world breaks everyone, and afterward, many are strong at the broken places."

– ERNEST HEMINGWAY, *A FAREWELL TO ARMS*

step away from the objects in the room
and place yourself on the Earth
close your eyes

what did you see?

now close them again

did you see red?

I did

before

when something like this happens
your life divides in two

before and after

and all at once, all that was left was after

violation

you made everyone laugh
you made me laugh
the class clown

Mr. Popular
in the good sense of the word

goofy
but smart and caring and gorgeous too

we loved you
I loved you

my best friend

there was blood
on my pants
it was crimson

my heart raced
swollen
with tears and excitement and rage

my skin screamed
let me
go
leave me
alone

go
I wish I had said

my arms
pinned to the sheets
cried
silently, not loud enough
to make it stop

my legs
quivered with frustration
not strong enough
to fling you from me

my body was sore
my heart was sore
my lungs were sore
from my silence

when my body stopped hurting
finally
my heart ached
deeper than I thought possible

my mind was the loudest it's ever been
yet it was
silent
at the same time

fourteen is too young
this can't be real
what happened
how did this happen
why did he do this
maybe I'm confused
I shouldn't have worn that
I allowed it to happen
why did this happen
how did this happen

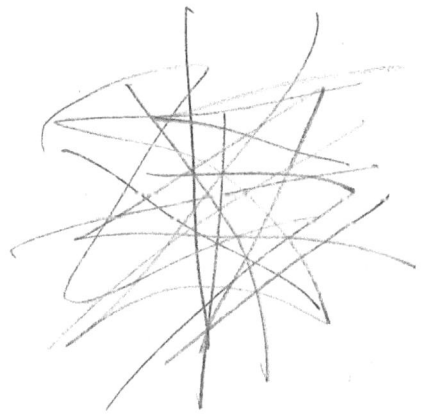

the thoughts whirled
around and around in my head
replaying each second
in slow motion

you made your case to me perfectly
you cared for me
you eased my pain
you held me

but this quickly turned
I was vulnerable
you were ready

I believed you could love me
how else could you comfort me that way

and the moment I began to trust
you violated me

your hands reached across my body
in places that had never been touched

you moved slowly
to allow me to warm up to the idea,
I suppose

when I returned your hands to safe spaces
you let me
you rested there

but when I let my guard down
those hands reached again

your hands
were sweaty and slimy and wrong

your hands
hurt my soul
exploring places they weren't meant to be

scarring my body

you had been drinking

maybe, you forgot what no meant
maybe, you were confused
maybe, you would stop

you didn't

suddenly it was no longer slow

hands
holding
wrists
down

hands
pushing
deeper
harder

hands
touching
feeling
stealing
from me

your fingers clawed
inside my body
scratching
violently

making me bleed out
red

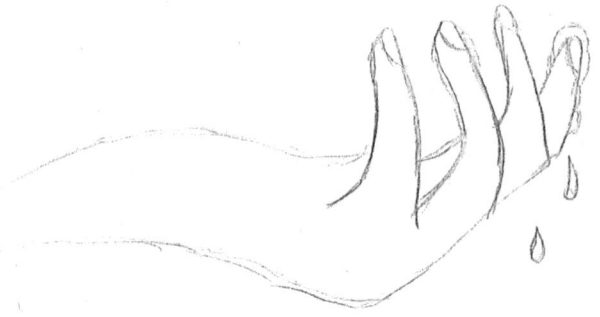

your eyes glanced over
they looked into mine
it was almost
romantic

they saw the tiny tear run down my cheek

and you were smiling
a big smile
goofy and pure
elusive and evil

did you know what you were doing?
did you care?

if you don't know who you are
you are a liar

you know
you did this to me

when I thought it was over
when I opened my eyes again to find the way out
I felt your hand inside me again

scraping my insides
digging into my body
taking from me what was not meant for sharing

stained
red was my heart

and my pants
and the sheets

your fingers were red, too

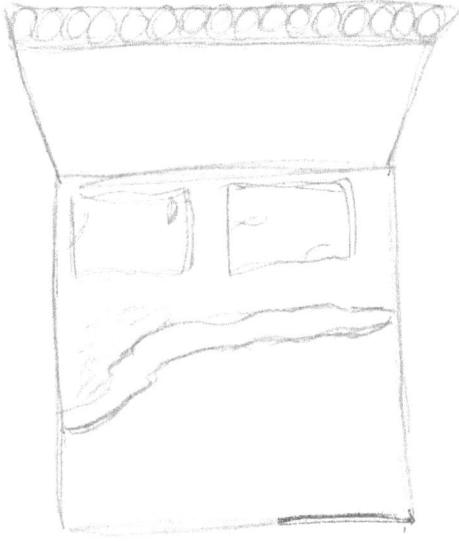

and when I left
you followed after me

grabbed my body
held me against you

hands
climbing
down
again

uninvited

the next day
your hands still molded on my wrists
gripping me all the same

I felt you in my bed
I was alone
but you lingered in my mind

I couldn't shake you then
I can't shake you now

no one had touched me that way before
felt my raw insides with their hands
put my being onto their skin

no one had seen my body in that way
so helpless and bare

each night in my sleep
I see your hands on my wrists
holding me down
smiling
telling me it feels good
telling me I feel good

congratulations, they said
you are a woman now

a man has touched you
don't you feel special?

we've all done it too,
they said

but it was different
they wanted this

I didn't

we were younger then
we didn't know
much more would come before us
that was
just the beginning

this has to end

five years later, I had taught myself to forget the feeling of your hands on my wrists, your fingers in my body, scraping my skin, I didn't remember the taste of your sweat dripping off your forehead onto my lips, I didn't see your grin in my mind when I closed my eyes. I didn't remember how long it took to end, how it seemed like forever, how each second was hours long with you holding me down, I forgot what I had worn, what day it was, what everyone said the next day at school when they had heard the news – she had been with a boy last night. I got new sheets, they were white, they were clean, my body wasn't red anymore. your hands were clean, you were no longer part of my past, you were forgotten, not something that came back to haunt me in my dreams, not someone that sat in the back of my mind.

but I learned these experiences are not unique. someone else, someone else I trusted, also explored my body, uninvited again. my wrists ached, no one should hold them, my body screamed, no one should enter uninvited, this one explored much deeper than the one before

he used his body.

everyone looked at you
as the ultimate conquest

you were older
you were beautiful
and smart
and so smooth

I caught your attention
I was the lucky one
you wanted me
you liked me
I was lucky

pushing in
my body wailed, the tiniest sound
I froze

red seeped out

when will it be over?

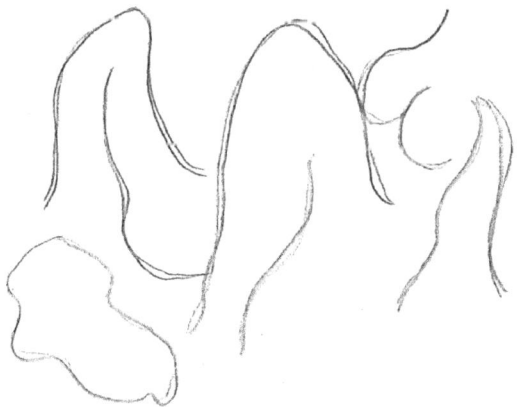

stop
I said
don't

ok
you said

you didn't stop

not once
has one entered by invitation

my veins wailed
innocence
lies here no more
his wailed, too
a different tune

I felt it in my stomach
and in my lungs

my thighs squeezed shut
not strong enough

I closed my eyes
waiting
for it to end
when will it end

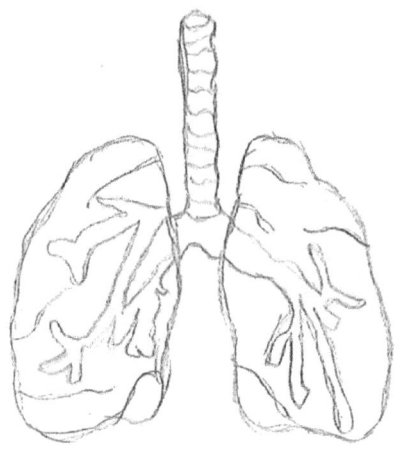

you moved faster
and faster
and faster

our breaths increasing
yours with pleasure
mine with fear

each push against my skin
against my will

your fingertips danced
through my hair
your lips traced
the veins of my neck

how could something so *romantic*
be so nauseating

and when your body began to slow
my breath followed
it must be over
it had to be over

but then it quickened
each push dragging my body
forward and backward
your hands holding me down

my eyes closed again
but I couldn't help but look
at your face

you enjoyed this

the rhythm
rocked my body back and forth
it shook my stomach

back forth
back forth
back forth
back forth

my lungs mimicked
the rhythm you instilled

inhale exhale
inhale exhale
inhale exhale

how could I give you this satisfaction

suddenly it stopped
I knew it was over then
I closed my eyes
maybe when I opened them you'd be gone

you stayed
you slept in my bed
you stayed with my being
spread across the sheets
red

I lay awake
wondering
how
to get back something that is gone ~~for good~~
for bad

you took something from me
I will never get back
it is gone now
forever

have you taken this from other girls
or am I the only one

why
was I chosen
how
did I deserve this

who else
has been violated?

the older girls
the younger girls
all felt him
inside and outside them

they didn't know my story
they didn't care
they loved attention
they loved him
they craved intimacy of the heart and soul
they got intimacy of the body

I am not the only one

hearing my story
from the mouth of another
and another and another
and another
is heartbreaking

I hurt for you

healing I

tell yourself
it didn't happen

eventually you will forget

I got it over with

it happened and now I can move on

like they said,
I am a woman now

I did like it
I was just confused

everyone likes it
everyone wants this
everyone is scared at first

I won't wear
the clothes that invite boys in
if I don't
they won't come

I won't go out
they can't get me
if I stay home

it will vanish
the way leaves turn red in the fall
and drop from trees
forever forgotten

I will forget

I can forget

nothing happened

and so I forgot

passion

you show up at my door
storm right through
pounce on my bed
to talk
tell me how your day was
all the intricacies
the irrelevant details

you are gorgeous
and smart
and everything I need

you are spontaneous
yet prepared
and invigorating

I love your presence
I love you

I didn't think I would love again
yet I always did

I didn't think I would feel again
yet I felt deeper than before

I didn't think I would love again
yet it continued to flow out of me

meeting you
was invigorating
you lit up my life

I could feel again

I am alive
I chase life
again
as I did before
when I was thirteen

you take me places
I have not seen
in a long time
you wake my soul

my mind wars with my heart
you should never love again
they can't be trusted
they can't be true
they can't be loved

but I love him

when you love someone
you cannot always resist
falling
into their grasp
into their control

loving someone is giving
your soul
completely and eternally

to you I gave
completely and eternally
the redness of my soul
all of me

it's you
it was always you
I'm just scared to admit that and end up alone

I would hate your flaws in anyone else but in you I see love
I see excitement
I see passion

your voice is ecstasy
it fills my lungs when you tell me
your dreams,
how I fit into them

you see the world
in color
yellow shines bright in your life
you are a light in my life
green is nature's wonders
you show me the beauty of simplicity
blue is the sky and the sea
you love the wonders of the world
red is passion and emotion

red is everything to me

it's you because you know my past
and you heal me with each touch and word

your skin grips mine
lightly and fully
we mold into one
covered in sheets and blankets, sweat and tears, heart and soul

your soul sets fire to mine
in a beautiful, red way

you make me feel
you make me curious
you make me love

you reach parts of me
that have never been reached before

touch me in that way
show me how to feel again
make me shiver
then warm my soul

whenever you are gone
I long for your touch
your smile
your soul

you call me by my name
you call me by my name
you call me by my name

no one else does that

say my name
again and again
and again
it makes me feel whole
it makes me feel me
you speak to me and not to my body
you speak to what's inside
and I answer in return

I love your smile
more than any in the world
when I see the edges of your lips curl up
mine do the same

you're painfully honest
that's how I know you mean it
when you whisper sweet nothings
quietly in my ear

when you speak it gives me butterflies
when you say you missed me I flush,
red

I fall deeper
and deeper
and deeper
in love with your soul
the way you make me feel

when he entered
I had already invited him
gently, he pleaded with my body
know that you are safe
know that I will not hurt you
know that you are loved

I am safe
I am not hurt
I am loved

I cried
innocence is not here
but beauty and grace are

be my first and know it
frighten me and mean everything
tell me I inspire you in ways no one has

sleep intertwined with my skin
pressed into yours like we are one

make my lips a part of your own
smile, your tongue belonging to my mouth

share my bed like it was your own
to make in the morning

I wish for it to stay that way
forever
but the seasons change
and so do our hearts

have you ever loved someone
who doesn't love you back?
my heart breaks
it only makes me love deeper

why is it this way?

come over
you come
into me
you leave

stay

if not now, then maybe not ever
will you plunge inside of me
knowing my skin completely
knowing my soul entirely

I lost you

my heart aches. you are all that I want. you are all that I need. but you are not what is good for me. you don't see value in me the way I see value in every inch of who you are. it's harder to lose someone who hasn't truly done you any wrong, but who doesn't love you the way that you need. that hurts more than a cheater. that hurts more than a liar.

you are a fool

your heart aches. I am all that you want. I am all that you need. but I am not what is good for you. I don't see value in you the way you see value in every inch of who I am. it's hardest to hurt someone who truly hasn't done you any wrong, but who you don't love the way that they need.

I hate hurting you

love is the hardest thing

you look back on it all
and maybe you can even pinpoint the falling to a day
you still don't really know how it happened
you just know you're glad it did

I'm glad it happened

not knowing
how you feel
is exciting

lightning strikes when you look at me

will this be
something I carry
or will this be
just another fleeting moment

red returns
to my heart
almost as quickly as it left

in a flash
it begins again

I didn't think I would love again
yet I always did

I didn't think I would feel again
yet I felt deeper than before

I didn't think I would love again
yet it continued to flow out of me

harm

the stresses start to grow
the calm fades away
thoughts swirl in my head every day and every night

the voices never stop
making me question

the feelings
cannot be explained
to myself or to you

the things in my head
are hard to say aloud

depression
anxiety
despair

they won't leave me

the voice in my head
rages on
suggesting my misery will not end

never a moment of silence

again and again
the voice repeats itself

drowning out the sound of life
forcing its own sound

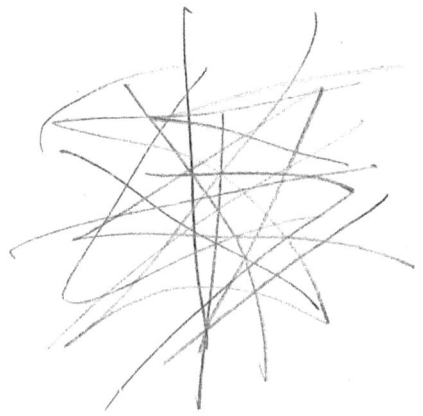

you are different
you do not fit
you have been violated
you are different
you do not fit
you have been violated
you are different
you do not fit
you have been violated

I am different
I do not fit
I have been violated

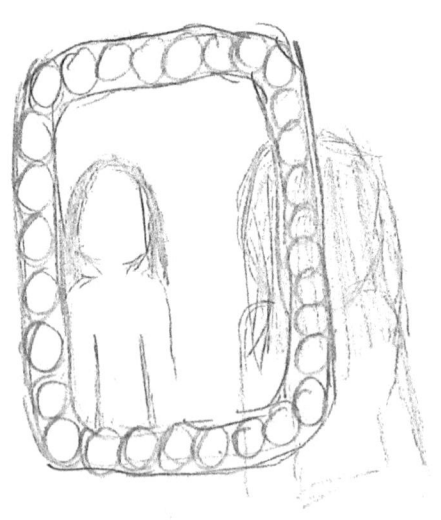

I keep this all in my head
no one knows I am different
no one knows I do not fit
no one knows I have been violated

everyone sees a girl who should be happy

why am I not happy?

I am so tired
sadness is exhausting

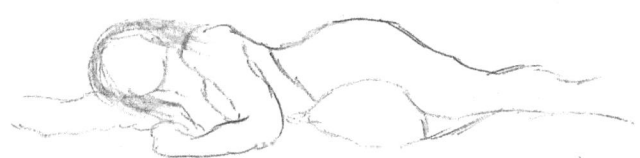

innocence
purity
cleanliness

are no longer mine

he stole that from me
again and again

each movement taking me farther from myself

I wanted to feel like her,
the girl that was violated
I wanted to know her pain
I wanted to know my pain

deep inside my skin
the way I had that day
the way so many have

it had to work
I needed to be engraved
with all of the moments
I am strong enough to dig deeper

red bled out
it didn't stop the numbness

I carved your scars carefully,
dangerously deep into my skin
in places no one would see
just as they didn't see what you did to me

the scars are mine

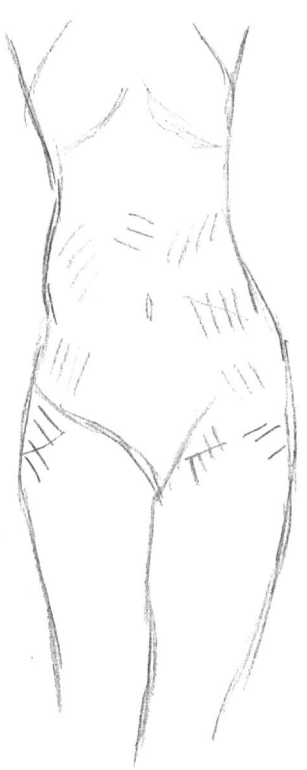

that was before I ever felt the pain
myself
and now I wish to take it back
give me back that innocence
give me back myself

the dagger that you used cut so deep
my insides seeped out onto the sheets
they are yours now

my knife traces the same lines that you once touched
I make the marks now
I am in control

I made myself bleed out
the color you had painted me
with your actions
with my blood

this will make my pain go away
I will feel again
I won't be numb anymore

come over
explore my body
use me
use my body for your pleasure
enjoy me

that's what boys want
that's what girls should do

if I do it
again and again
making it normal
it won't hurt anymore
I won't feel it
it will be normal

everyone else does it
I should too

I let them
I give them my body

I am naked
I am bare
I give completely
with no emotional exchange

I am covered
fully
I am not vulnerable

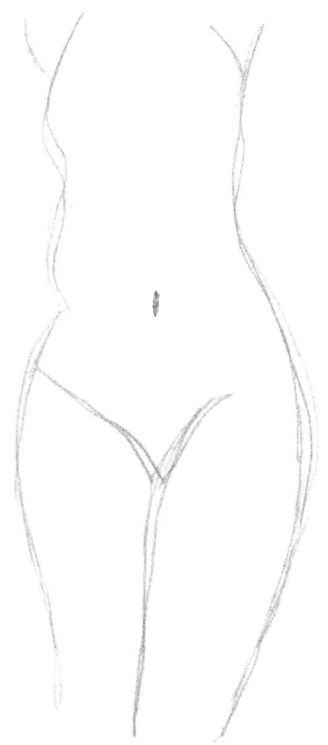

therapy will help
they say

it will heal you
it will make you feel again

I don't want to be someone who needs therapy

I don't want to be here
I didn't tell her
but she knew

she doesn't say anything
just watches
with a pen and paper

she studies me
I study the floor

we talk
about my parents
they love me
they are hurting too
they don't understand
why I am struggling

it's not fair
I am hurting more

one day
I want to talk
I want to tell her
I want to say it

the words are hard
they don't come
the way they rattle in my head

my voice is taken from me

I always thought
it must have been the clothes I wore
I must have given some confused signal
I could have done something different

it is not your fault

those words
sink deep into my skin
I didn't ask for this
it is not my fault

it is not your fault

the therapist tells me
it could be you
the reason why

I don't sleep at night
I shake in the day
I cry when I'm happy

you are the reason

my
wrists
can't
be
touched

you are the fear
that lives inside me
you are the reason
I am scared
an ugly shade of red

I see it all again in my sleep

every night
you crawl toward me
your claws waiting to dig in
your lips pursed with desire

I hate sleeping
but I am so tired

I sleep in the day
at night you haunt me
in the day, I am alone in my slumber

when did it become something we had to do?
when did it stop happening on its own?
I had never known love to be a tiresome act

I get jealous
I was never that way
what happened to me?

I don't like to see you with her
I know you are just friends
bitterness sweeps into my veins
I put on blush
and do my hair
I go to bed

alone

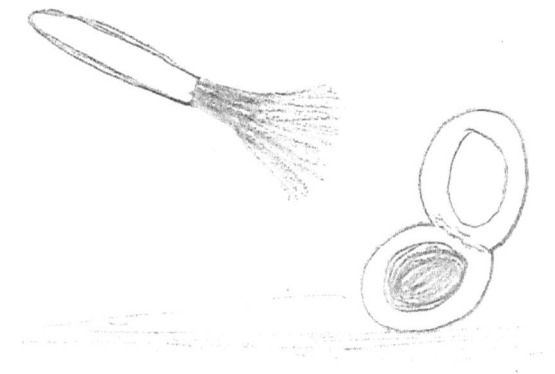

I gain a pound every day since then
sometimes I cry them off
other times they stay on

if my body is less desirable
only those who truly care for me
will touch the crevices

the rest will stay away

always running
is tiring

I want to be still

those you love
are supposed to comfort you
my parents make me feel safe

how can I tell them?

parents like to heal
they want to fix

how do I tell them
they cannot fix this

telling them hurts me
how can I engrave my deepest scar in them
they cannot keep me safe

I don't want to hurt them
but I need their comfort
I need their understanding
I am different now

this will always
be part of me
it will never go away

it is who I am

healing II

there is no way to say
what happened
words cannot say
what races through my head

it took over a year
to utter the word
the word that means what you did to me

it is a big word
that does not have to be said
for it to be felt

Rapidly entering my soul
  Attacking my insides
    Personally destroying my mind
      Eternally engraved in my skin

let me just say it

it is, at best
a form of assault

unlucky

someone grant me the serenity to accept the things I cannot change

I didn't know
that it was wrong
for someone to touch pieces of you
that you wanted kept private

what they did
is
not
okay

I know that now

it's not your fault,
they tell me
it's not your fault
it's not your fault
it's not your fault

now I believe them

this
is
not
my
fault

my soul stayed red
with distrust and blood

you are not me
you are not my story
you are not gone

each step
is coupled with the understanding
that I may have to retreat
before I can soar

did you feel
the way I felt that night
warm and excited

in a way that makes you nauseous and angry and scared and sad
and broken all at the same time?

did you know my inside?

I don't think you really did

you can't without me allowing it
all you felt was skin
only I know my inside

only I
write my story
what you did
does not define me
it cannot take away
from who I am

I am stronger
because of your mistakes

the biggest mistakes
deserve to be
remembered
celebrated
and learned from

I will learn from you
we all will learn
together
we will change this

it ends now

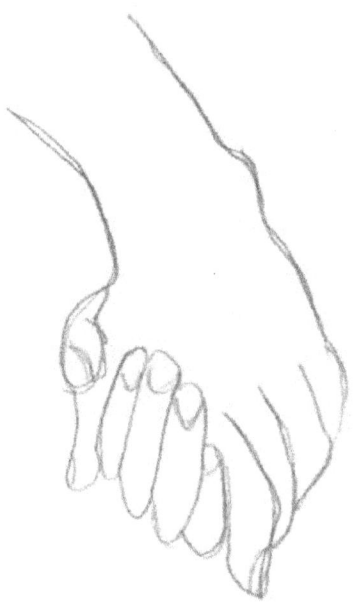

my words make me powerful
I will hold this over you
in these pages, forever
you cannot take this from me

the redness of my soul is
mine
it cannot be hushed

my words will never be erased
the way you tried
to erase my voice
yelling stop
my body
pleading for release

you
have
no
power
over
me

my words will never be erased

enjoy the silence of the morning
it looms with peace

a new day has come
a new beginning for those of us who seek one

a new day
is only a day away

take this day
use it
let it make you stronger

it is not selfish to take care of yourself

I am worthy

say those words aloud
I am worthy

healing is an eternal process

it is time
that we speak up
speak out
speak loud

let our redness show

we are powerful
we are strong

be everything that you are
be red
for me

but especially, for you.

special thanks

to everyone who preordered this book
and believed in me
I am eternally grateful for your support

Betsy Foster
Jay Foster*
Dibby Griffin
Griffin Foster
Riley Hill
Michelle Tobias
Betty Hewell
Eric Koester
Avery Robinson
Chris Burke
Keri Shaw
Elizabeth Bradshaw
Misti Robinson
Mark & Oni Strawn
Maggie White
Beth Roberts
Mary Ann Frishman
Cira Mancuso
Kimberly Bernstein
Maria Brummer
Elizabeth Henneke
Barsa Harclerode

Alexandra George
Olivia McClay
Rod Mitchell
Eliza Quincy
Loretta Mitchell
Jill Jones*
Emma Powless
Dana Brimmer
James Jones
Rachel Atler
Liza Layne
Kristin Pichler
Isabel Pichler
Dan Garrison
Doug Jones*
Abigail Garnick*
Angela Benkendorfer
Dani Daily
Blake Trahan
Beth Sherwood
Jim Sud*
Anne Smalling*

Bill Griffin

Jennifer Hancock

Chris Fehr

Cole Baker

Lecia Sud

Sandy Hill

Scott Arnold

Cherie Hendershot

Katherine Baker

Linnea Schuessler

Katie Hindes

William Neighbors

Emily Gaddie

Susan Logan

Nancie Chapman

Celia McNair

Rita Keenan

Carole Cain

Nicole Elliott

Mary Margaret Johnson

Keely Moran

Lea Steinberger

Diana Patterson

Molly Sherman

The Trahan Family*

Mackenzie Finklea

Bonnie Arnold

Hanna Brown

Karen Brimble

Robyn Gill

Don Livingston

Kelsey Hendershot*

The McCann Family

Anne Smalling*

Josie Toubin*

Karla Bell

Tracy Barton*

Karen Hunt

Morgan Roder

Caitlin Babb

Eileen Paliakas

Griff Griffin*

Mary Alice Sherman

Lisa & Bob Wade

Elizabeth Schultz*

Joan Swartz

Laura Grim

Jennifer Mouritsen*

Missy Mouritsen

Elizabeth Bray

Julie Ballard*

Leslie Ireland*

Margaret Roberts

Cynthia Smith*

Noor Alahmadi

Olivia Smith

Isaiah Castillo

Rodney Woodley

Laura Wieland

Cecelia Abbott

Marcy Greer*

Holly McDonald

Kellie O'Brien

Cat Cummins

Ainslie Tisdale

Katie Romano

Michelle Chin

Tisa Foster

Bhaargavi Ashok

Allison Baker

Aimee Williams

Perla Aguirre

Vlad Wallace

Nicole Wojtkiewicz

Stephanie Markham

Benjamin Rubanov

Sofia Wicks

Gavin Downing

www.ingramcontent.com/pod-product-compliance
Lightning Source LLC
Chambersburg PA
CBHW071523180526
45171CB00002B/356